·My·First·
Dictionary

Illustrated by
Alan
Snow

FUNK & WAGNALLS EDITION

Aa

above

If something is **above** you, it is higher than you are.

across

When you go **across** something, you go from one side to the other.

address

Aunt Agnes
16 Florida Drive
Anytown
15600

Your **address** is where you live. Your house, street, town, and country make up your **address**.

airplane

An **airplane** is a machine that flies in the air. **Airplanes** have wings and engines.

alphabet

abcdefghijKl
mnopqrstuvwxyz

An **alphabet** is a list of all the letters that make words.

angry

If you are **angry**, you are mad at or unhappy with someone.

animal

An **animal** is any living thing except a plant. People, dogs, fish, flies, and snails are all **animals**.

answer

Yes please!

If someone calls you or asks you a question, what you say next is your **answer**.

apple

An **apple** is a round fruit that grows on a tree. **Apples** can have red, yellow, or green skin.

asleep

When you are **asleep**, you are resting. You don't know what is going on around you.

awake

When you are **awake**, you are not sleeping. Your eyes are open, and you notice things around you.

Bb

baby

A **baby** is a very young boy or girl.

bad

1. A **bad** person is someone who hurts others in some way.

2. **Bad** food is not fit to eat.

bag
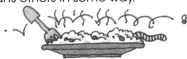
A **bag** is made to carry or hold things. **Bags** are usually soft.

bake

When people **bake** food, they cook it in an oven.

ball
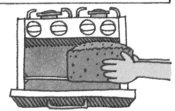
A **ball** is a round object used in lots of games.

balloon

A **balloon** is a bag filled with air or gas that makes it float.

Bb

bark

1. The **bark** of a tree is its skin.

2. The loud noise that a dog makes is its **bark**.

bat

1. A **bat** is a strong, often wooden stick used in some games.

2. A **bat** is also a small, furry animal, like a mouse with wings. **Bats** fly mostly at night.

bath

A **bath** is a container big enough to wash your whole body in.

beach

The **beach** is the land along the edge of the ocean. It usually has sand or small stones on it.

bean

A **bean** is a flat, smooth seed eaten as a vegetable. **Beans** are found inside long pods.

bear

A **bear** is a big, heavy animal. It has thick fur and strong claws.

bed

A **bed** is something to lie on when you rest or sleep.

bee

A **bee** is a flying insect. **Bees** make honey and wax.

below

If something is **below** you, it is lower than you are.

bicycle

A **bicycle** has two wheels. You can ride it by sitting on it and turning the pedals with your feet.

big

If something is **big**, it is great in size or amount.

bird

A **bird** is an animal with wings and feathers. Most **birds** can fly. Baby **birds** come from eggs.

birthday

Your **birthday** is a special day that you remember every year, because it was the day that you were born.

boat

A **boat** carries people and things on water. A motor, sails, paddles, or oars make it go.

body

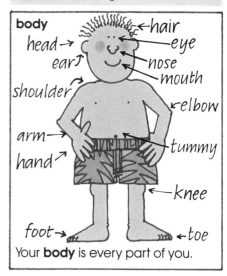

Your **body** is every part of you.

book

A **book** is made of pieces of paper attached together down one side. **Books** often tell a story.

bottle

A **bottle** is usually made of glass or plastic. It is for holding things that you can pour, such as orange juice and cough syrup.

Bb

bottom

The **bottom** of something is its lowest part.

bowl

A **bowl** is a dish that's round and has an open top. It holds things such as food.

box

A **box** has straight sides and holds things such as toys. It often comes with a lid or top.

boy

A **boy** is a child who will be a man when he grows up.

brave

If you are **brave**, you can face pain or danger without fear.

bread

Bread is a food. It is made with flour and baked in an oven.

break

If you **break** something, it falls apart, or stops working.

breakfast

Breakfast is the food you eat first thing in the morning.

bridge

A **bridge** is a road that crosses a river, a railroad, or a highway.

build

If you **build** something, you make it by putting things together.

bus

A **bus** carries a lot of people along the road.

butterfly

A **butterfly** is an insect with four brightly colored wings.

buy

When you **buy** something, you get it by giving money for it.

Cc

can

1. If you say you **can** do something, that means you are able to do it.

2. A **can** is used to keep things in or fresh, such as food. **Cans** are often made of metal.

car

A **car** is made to take a few people along roads.

carrot

A **carrot** is a vegetable. Its long, orange root grows underground.

carry

If you **carry** something, you lift it and take it with you.

cat

A **cat** is an animal with short ears and a long tail.

catch

If you **catch** something, you get hold of it while it is moving.

chair

A **chair** is something to sit on.

Cc

chase

If you **chase** somebody, you run after them to try to catch them.

cheese

Cheese is a food. It is made from milk.

chick

A **chick** is a young bird that has just come out of the egg.

circus

A **circus** is a place where you can see trained animals, acrobats, and clowns perform.

city

A **city** is a very large place with a lot of buildings. Many people live and work in **cities**.

clean

If something is **clean**, it has no dirt on it.

climb

If you **climb** something like a tree, you go up it, using your hands and feet.

clock

A **clock** is something that shows you what the time is.

clothes

Your **clothes** are all the things that you wear to cover you and keep you warm.

cloud

Clouds are made up of tiny drops of water. They are gray or white and float high up in the sky.

cold

1. If the weather is **cold**, you need to wear a coat outside.

2. If you have a **cold**, you feel sick. **Colds** cause sneezing, coughing, and blocked or runny noses.

color

Red, blue, yellow, and green are all **colors**. There are a lot of different **colors**.

cook

When someone **cooks** food, they get it ready to eat by making it hot.

cookie

A **cookie** is a small, flat kind of cake that tastes sweet.

count

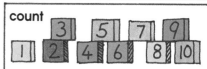

When you **count** things, you find out how many of them there are.

country

1. A **country** is a very large place. The United States is a **country**.

2. The **country** is land away from cities and most towns. There are trees and farms in the **country**.

cow

A **cow** is a big female farm animal that can give milk.

Cc

crawl

If you **crawl**, you move along on your hands and knees.

crayon

Crayons are colored wax sticks for drawing or writing.

cross

1. A **cross** is a shape made by two lines, sometimes like this.

2. If you **cross** something like a street, you go from one side to the other.

cup

A **cup** is something that you can drink from. Some **cups** have handles.

cut

1. If you **cut** yourself, it hurts and you bleed.

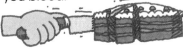

2. If you **cut** a cake, you make it into smaller pieces.

Dd

dance

When you **dance**, you move your whole body in a special way. People often **dance** to music.

dark

1. When it is **dark**, you cannot see very well because there is not enough light.

2. **Dark** hair is brown or black.

day

1. Your **day** is the time between getting up and going to bed.

2. A **day** is also part of a week. There are seven **days** in one week.

Monday Tuesday Wednesday Thursday Friday Saturday Sunday

decide

When you **decide** to do something, you make up your mind about it.

deer

A **deer** is a large, fast animal. Many **deer** have horns called antlers. **Deer** eat leaves and grass.

different

If two things are **different**, they are not like each other in one or more ways.

dig

When you **dig**, you make a hole in something such as earth or sand.

dinner

Dinner is the biggest or main meal of the day.

dirty

Something that is **dirty** is not clean. Things that are **dirty** need to be cleaned.

dish

A **dish** is a plate or nearly flat bowl to put food on.

dive

If you **dive** into the water, you jump in headfirst.

dog

A **dog** is a four-legged animal that barks. There are many different kinds of **dogs**.

door

A **door** is a way into a house or a room. **Doors** open and close. Some **doors** swing, and some slide.

draw

When you **draw**, you make a pattern or a picture of something. You can **draw** with anything that will make a mark, such as a pencil, a pen, or a crayon.

dream

Dreams are things that happen in your mind when you are asleep.

dry

Something that is **dry** has no water in it at all.

duck

A **duck** is a bird that spends a lot of time in the water. **Ducks** have webbed feet so that they can swim well.

ear

Your **ear** is part of your body. You have one **ear** on each side of your head. You use your **ears** to hear sounds.

early

1. The **early** part of something is near the beginning of it. *They decided to get up **early** in the morning.*

2. If you get somewhere **early**, you are there before the time arranged. *They were a little **early** and had to wait for the show to start.*

earth

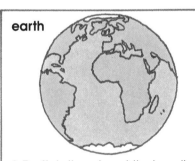

1. **Earth** is the planet that we live on. It is one of the nine planets that go around the sun.

2. **Earth** is also the ground that plants grow in.

eat

When you **eat**, you put food in your mouth. Then you chew it and swallow it.

egg

An **egg** is a round object laid by female birds, insects, snakes, and fish. A baby bird grows in an **egg** until it is ready to be born.

elephant

An **elephant** is a very large, heavy animal. **Elephants** have big ears and a long nose called a trunk. An **elephant** can pick things up with its trunk.

empty

If something like a box or a bottle is **empty**, it has nothing in it.

explain

When you **explain** something, you talk about it so that people will understand.

eye

An **eye** is part of your body. Your **eyes** are in the front of your head. You see things with your **eyes**.

Ff

face

Your **face** is the front part of your head. Your eyes, nose, mouth, cheeks, and chin are all part of your **face**.

fair

1. A **fair** is a place where people can buy and sell things, and have fun.

2. Something that is **fair** seems right to most people.

fall

1. If you **fall**, you suddenly drop toward the ground.

2. The **fall** is a time of year between summer and winter. In the **fall**, leaves begin to **fall** from the trees.

farm

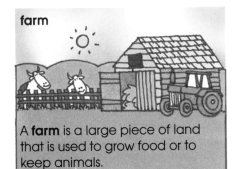

A **farm** is a large piece of land that is used to grow food or to keep animals.

fast

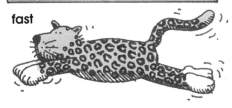

People or things that are **fast** can move very quickly.

favorite

Your **favorite** is the one you like best. *This is my favorite doll.*

feather

Feathers are the very light things that cover a bird's body and wings.

feel

1. The way you **feel** is how you are at the time. You might **feel** happy, excited, or sad.

2. When you **feel** something, you know you are touching it, or it is touching you. Fur **feels** soft, sandpaper **feels** rough, and snow **feels** cold.

find

When you **find** something, you usually come upon the thing you were looking for.

fire

Fire is the hot flames that come from something burning.

fish

A **fish** is an animal that lives in the water. **Fish** have fins and a tail. There are many different kinds of **fish**. Some are good to eat.

fit

If clothes **fit**, they are the right size for you. They are not too large or too small.

fix

When people **fix** things, they make them work again.

float

When things **float**, they move on top of the water.

floor

The **floor** of a room is the part that you walk on.

flower

A **flower** is part of a plant. **Flowers** are very pretty.

Ff

fly

1. Things that **fly** move through the air. Most birds can **fly**. If we want to **fly** somewhere, we usually go in an airplane.

2. A **fly** is a small insect with wings.

follow

When you **follow** somebody, you go after them.

food

Food is what we eat. People, animals, and plants all need **food** to help them grow.

fork

A **fork** is something you use to eat food with. It is long and has three or four thin pointed parts on its end.

fox

A **fox** is a wild animal that looks something like a dog. It has a bushy tail and thick fur.

free

If something is **free**, you do not have to pay any money to get it.

friend

A **friend** is someone you like very much. A **friend** likes being with you, too.

frog

A **frog** is a small animal that spends a lot of time in the water. **Frogs** can jump a long way.

fruit

A **fruit** is the part of a plant that has seeds and can be eaten. Apples and grapes are **fruits**.

full

If something is **full**, it will not hold any more.

funny

Something that is **funny** makes you laugh.

fur

Fur is thick hair that grows on an animal's body. **Fur** keeps animals warm.

Gg

game

A **game** is something you play. Hide-and-seek is a **game**.

garden

A **garden** is a place where flowers or vegetables are grown. Many **gardens** are near people's homes.

girl

A **girl** is a child who will be a woman when she grows up.

good

1. A person who is **good** is kind and caring.

2. If you say something such as food or a show was **good**, you mean you enjoyed it.

grass

Grass is a green plant. It has thin leaves that grow closely together. You can see **grass** in lawns and in fields.

grow

When living things **grow**, they get larger.

Hh

hair

Hair looks like very thin threads growing on your skin. Many animals, such as dogs, grow **hair**.

half

If you cut something in **half**, you cut it into two parts that are the same size.

happy

When you are **happy**, you feel very good. That's because something nice has happened or because things are the way you want them to be.

hard

1. If something is **hard**, you cannot push your fingers into it. Rocks are **hard**.

$$345123 \times 234 =$$

2. If you say something was **hard** to do, you mean you had to work at it or give it a lot of effort.

hat

A **hat** is something to wear on your head.

hear

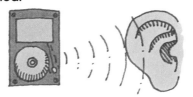

When you can **hear** something, sounds are coming into your ears.

heavy

Something that is **heavy** is hard to pick up.

help

When you **help** somebody, you do something for them.

hide

If you **hide** something, you put it where it can't be seen.

high

Something that is **high** in the air is a long way off the ground.

hill

A **hill** is land that is higher than the land around it.

hit

If you **hit** something, you touch or come against it hard.

hole

A **hole** is an opening or hollow place in something. *The dog was about to jump through the fence* **hole**.

horse

A **horse** is a big, four-legged animal that people can ride.

Hh

hot

1. If something is **hot**, it burns when you touch it.

2. If you feel **hot**, you are too warm.

hour

An **hour** is part of a day. There are twenty-four **hours** in one day.

house

A **house** is a building for people to live in.

hungry

When you are **hungry**, you feel you want something to eat.

hurt

If you **hurt** part of your body, it feels sore.

Ii

ice

Ice is frozen water. When water turns into **ice**, it becomes solid and you can't pour it.

idea

When people have an **idea**, they think of a way of doing something.

important

Someone or something that is **important** matters a lot.

insect

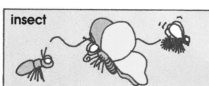

An **insect** is a very small animal with six legs. Most **insects** have wings. Ants and butterflies are **insects**.

inside

The **inside** of something is the part that has a covering around it.

invite

When you **invite** someone to your party, you ask them to come.

island

An **island** is a piece of land that has water all around it.

Jj

join

1. When you **join** two things, you put them together.

2. If you **join** a group, you become a member.

joke

A **joke** is something funny. People tell **jokes** or do things as a **joke** to make you laugh.

juice

Juice is a liquid. You can get **juice** from fruit such as oranges. You squeeze the orange and the **juice** comes out.

jump

When you **jump**, you throw yourself into the air.

Kk

key

A **key** is a small piece of metal that can open or close a lock. *Use the key to open the iron box.*

kick

When you **kick** something, you hit it with your foot.

kiss

If you **kiss** somebody, you touch them with your lips.

kite

A **kite** is a light toy. You can fly a **kite** in the wind on the end of a long string.

kitten

A **kitten** is a baby cat.

knife

A **knife** is something sharp that you can cut with.

knock

When you **knock** something, you hit it. You **knock** at a door when you want someone to come.

knot

You tie a **knot** in a piece of string when you want to join two ends together.

Ll

ladder

Ladders are steps you can move from place to place. **Ladders** are used for climbing up things.

lake

A **lake** is a lot of fresh water with land all around it.

land

1. **Land** is the part of the earth that is not covered by the oceans. We live on the **land**.

2. When an airplane **lands**, it comes down to the ground.

late

1. The **late** part of something is near the end of it. *The party ended late in the afternoon.*

2. If you are **late**, you get to a place after the time you were supposed to be there. *I was late for school today.*

lead

When you **lead**, you go in front of other people.

learn

When you **learn** something, you get to know it.

left

Everything has a **left** side and a right side. The **left** side of a page is the side that you begin reading on in English.

letter

1. A **letter** is a shape such as **A** or **C** that stands for a sound. You use **letters** to make words.

2. A **letter** is also a written message you send to somebody.

lick

If you **lick** something, you touch it with your tongue.

lift

When you **lift** something, you pick it up.

light

1. **Light** is a form of energy that lets us see. The sun, candles, and lamps all give off **light**.

2. Something that is **light** has little weight and is easy to lift.

Ll

like

If you **like** somebody or something, that person or thing makes you happy.

lion

A **lion** is a big, strong, wild cat.

lonely

If you feel **lonely**, you are unhappy because you are by yourself.

lose

If you **lose** something, you can't find it anywhere.

loud

Something that is **loud** makes a lot of noise.

love

If you **love** someone, you like them very much.

low

Something that is **low** is close to the ground or below the usual level.

lunch

Lunch is a meal that you eat in the middle of the day.

Mm

magic

In stories, **magic** makes impossible things happen. Some people can do tricks, which look like **magic**. They can make things appear and disappear.

make

When you **make** something, you build it. *Shall we **make** a box out of paper?*

man

A **man** is an adult male person. A boy grows up to be a **man**.

meal

A **meal** is food that people eat at certain times of the day. Breakfast and dinner are **meals**.

measure

You can **measure** something to find out how big or heavy it is. *Use your ruler to **measure** that piece of paper.*

meat

Meat is parts of an animal that are used for food.

melt

When ice cubes **melt**, they change back into water.

milk

Milk is a white liquid food you can drink. The **milk** we drink usually comes from cows.

minute

A **minute** is part of an hour. There are sixty **minutes** in one hour.

mix

When you **mix** different things, you put them together. You **mix** flour, butter, sugar, and eggs to make a cake.

money

Money is something you use to buy things with. Dollars, nickels, and dimes are **money**.

monkey

A **monkey** is an animal that lives in places where there are lots of trees. They have strong hands and long tails to help them swing through the tree branches.

Mm

month

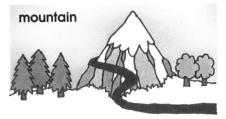

A **month** is part of a year. There are twelve **months** in one year.

moon

The **moon** is the pale yellow ball that gives light in the sky at night. The **moon** moves from west to east around the earth.

mountain

A **mountain** is land that is a lot higher than the land around it.

mouse

A **mouse** is a small, furry animal. **Mice** have long tails.

mouth

Your **mouth** is the place you put food into when you eat. You also use your **mouth** to make words and sounds.

music

Music is made up of special sounds that are nice to hear. The sounds are made by such things as a piano or a guitar.

Nn

name

A **name** is a word that you call somebody or something by. *Our new baby's **name** is Joe.*

near

If something is **near** you, it is not very far away.

nest

A **nest** is a home that a bird makes for its babies.

new

When something is **new**, it has not been used before.

nice

Something **nice** is something that you like.

night

Night is the time when it is dark outside.

nose

Your **nose** is the part that sticks out in the middle of your face. You use your **nose** for smelling and breathing.

number

A **number** is a symbol or word that can tell you how many things there are. *The **number** of fingers here is five.*

Oo

ocean

An **ocean** is a very, very large area of water. Fish and other animals live in the **ocean**.

old

1. Someone who is **old** has lived for a long time.

2. Something **old** has been used a lot.

open

When something is **open**, you can go in and out of it, or get at the things inside.

orange

An **orange** is a round fruit with thick skin and sweet juice.

outside

The **outside** of something is the part that you can see without opening it.

over

1. If something is **over** something else, it is above it.

2. If we say the play is **over**, we mean it is finished.

owl

An **owl** is a bird with large, round eyes that makes hooting sounds and usually hunts at night.

Pp

pack

When you **pack**, you put things in a suitcase or box.

paint

Paint is something you use to color things.

pair

A **pair** is made up of two things that go together, such as a **pair** of shoes.

paper

Paper is something to write on or wrap things in.

party

A **party** is a lot of people who come together to have a good time.

pen

A **pen** is a tool for writing in ink.

pencil

You can use a **pencil** for writing or drawing. **Pencils** make marks that you can rub out easily with an eraser.

pet

A **pet** is an animal that you keep in your home.

phone

A **phone** is something you can use for talking to someone who is far away from you. The word **phone** is short for "telephone."

picture

A **picture** shows what something looks like.

pie

A **pie** is a dessert that is cooked for you to eat. **Pies** can have fruit in them.

pig

A **pig** is a short, heavy animal kept on a farm.

plant

A **plant** is a living thing that grows in the earth.

play

1. When you **play**, you do something for fun.

2. If you **play** a piano, you make music with it.

pocket

A **pocket** is a little bag sewn on or into your clothes.

potato

A **potato** is a round vegetable growing underground.

pour

If you **pour** something like water, you make it flow from one place to another.

present

A **present** is something special that you give to someone.

pretend

When you **pretend**, you make believe something is real. *Let's pretend to be cowboys.*

pretty

Something **pretty** is nice to look at.

Pp

prize

A **prize** is something won or earned in a contest or game.

promise

If you **promise** to do something, you mean you will do it.

pull

If you **pull** something, you grab and move it toward you.

puppy

A **puppy** is a baby dog.

push

If you **push** something, you press on it to move it away from you.

puzzle

A **puzzle** is something that you have to think about hard in order to figure out. It can be a game, like a crossword **puzzle** or a picture **puzzle**.

Qq

question

What is the time?

Someone who asks a **question** is trying to find something out.

quick

Someone or something that is **quick** is very fast.

quiet

If you are **quiet**, you do not make any noise.

Rr

rabbit

A **rabbit** is a small furry animal with long ears and a small tail.

race

A **race** is a way to find out who goes the fastest.

radio

A **radio** can pick up sounds from the air. You can turn on a **radio** and listen to voices and music.

Rr

rain

Rain is water that drops from clouds in the sky.

rainbow

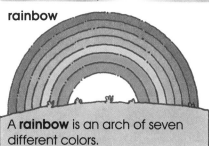

A **rainbow** is an arch of seven different colors.

read

When you can **read**, you can look at words and know what they mean.

ready

When you are **ready** to do something, you have all the things you need.

rest

When you **rest**, you stop what you are doing and sit or lie down for a while.

right

1. Most people draw with their **right** hand.

2. If something is **right**, it does not have any mistakes in it.

ring

1. A **ring** is something round, like a circle.

2. A **ring** is also a clear sound, like that of a bell.

river

A **river** is water that flows across the land.

road

A **road** is a way to get from place to place. Cars and buses go on **roads**.

roof

A **roof** is the cover on top of a house.

run

When you **run**, you move on your feet as fast as you can.

sad

When you are **sad**, you are unhappy about something.

same

If two things are the **same**, they are alike.

school

Most children go to **school** to learn things.

scissors

A pair of **scissors** is something you can use to cut paper and cloth.

see

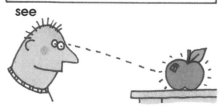

When you **see**, you look at something with your eyes.

seed

A **seed** is a very small part of a plant. New plants grow from **seeds**.

sell

If someone **sells** you something, they give it to you in exchange for money.

sheep

A **sheep** is a four-legged animal. **Sheep** have thick wool coats.

shout

A **shout** is a loud cry you make when you want somebody to hear you.

show

1. When you **show** something, you let people see it.

2. A **show** is something you can watch at a theater or circus. You can also watch **shows** on TV.

shut

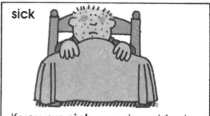

If you **shut** something like a door, you close it.

sick

If you are **sick**, you do not feel well.

sign

A **sign** is a mark or words that tell you something.

Ss

sing

When you **sing**, you make music with your voice.

sky

The **sky** is the space above you when you are outdoors.

sleep

When you **sleep**, you rest with your eyes closed. You don't know what is going on around you.

slow

People and animals that are **slow** don't move very fast.

small

Creatures or things that are **small** are little in size. *Ants and worms are small.*

smell

When you **smell** something, you're aware of it through your nose.

smile

When you **smile**, the corners of your mouth go up. You look happy when you **smile**.

snow

Snow is frozen rain. **Snow** falls from the sky in little pieces called snowflakes.

soap

Soap is something that you use with water to help make things clean.

soft
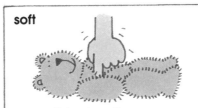

If something is **soft**, you can push your fingers into it easily.

sound

A **sound** is anything that you can hear.

spoon

A **spoon** has a small, shallow bowl at its end for eating.

spring

Spring is the time of year between winter and summer.

stairs

Stairs are steps that you go up and down in a house.

star

A **star** is a tiny light that you can see in the sky at night.

start

When you **start** doing something, you begin to do it.

stop

If you **stop** doing something, you don't do it for a while.

story

A **story** is something that people tell about things that have happened. A **story** can be about real things, or it can be made up.

summer

Summer is the time of year between spring and fall.

sun

The **sun** shines in the sky in the daytime. The **sun** gives us light and keeps us warm.

swim

When you **swim**, you move in the water and stay afloat by using your arms and legs.

Tt

table
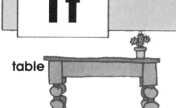
A **table** is something with a flat top to put things on.

talk
When you **talk**, you say words that people will understand.

taste

You **taste** things when you put them in your mouth.

teach

When someone **teaches** you, they help you learn how to do something.

teeth

Teeth are the hard, white things in your mouth. You use your **teeth** to bite and chew your food.

throw
When you **throw** something, you send it through the air.

tiger

A **tiger** is a big cat that often has orange fur with black stripes.

top

The **top** of something is the highest part of it.

towel

A **towel** is something you use to dry yourself.

town
A **town** is a place where there are houses and other buildings. People live and work in **towns**.

toy

A **toy** is something that you can play with.

train

A **train** is a lot of railroad cars joined together in a line. An engine pulls the **train** along.

tree

A **tree** is a very tall plant. The main part of a **tree** is called a trunk.

truck

A **truck** is like a big car. **Trucks** carry big or heavy things.

TV

A **TV** picks up pictures from the air. You can watch the pictures on a **TV**.

Uu

ugly

Things that are **ugly** are not nice to look at.

umbrella

An **umbrella** is something you hold over your head to keep the rain or the sun off of you.

under

If something is **under** you, it is lower than you are.

Vv

valley

A **valley** is the low land between hills or mountains.

vegetable

A **vegetable** is a plant that you can eat. Carrots, onions, and potatoes are **vegetables**.

visit

If someone **visits** you, they come to see you.

Ww

walk

When you **walk**, you move along on your feet without running.

warm

You wear **warm** things to stop you from feeling cold.

wash

When you **wash** something, you make it clean by using soap and water.

watch

1. When you **watch** something, you look at it for some time.

2. A **watch** is a small clock that you can wear.

water

Water is something you drink and wash with. It also falls from the sky as rain and fills rivers, lakes, and oceans.

weather

The **weather** is what it is like outdoors. You wear a coat if the **weather** is cold.

week

A **week** is seven days. There are fifty-two **weeks** in a year.

wet

If something is **wet**, it has water on it or in it.

wind

When there is a **wind**, the air moves, and things like leaves blow around.

window

A **window** is a place in a wall where the light can come in. **Windows** have glass in them.

wing

The **wings** of a bird or an insect are the parts of its body that it uses to fly with. Airplanes need **wings**, too.

winter

Winter is the time of the year between fall and spring.

woman

A **woman** is an adult female person. A girl grows up to be a **woman**.

word

Words are the things you use when you speak or write.

write

When you **write**, you put words on something like paper.

Xx

x-ray

An **x-ray** is a picture of the inside of somebody. Doctors use **x-rays** to see if any bones are broken.

Yy

yawn

When you **yawn**, you open your mouth very wide and take a deep breath. You sometimes **yawn** if you are sleepy.

year

A **year** is the same as 12 months, or 52 weeks, or 365 days.

young

Someone who is **young** has not been alive very long.

Zz

zipper

A **zipper** is a way of holding things together. Some clothes and bags have **zippers** on them.

zoo

A **zoo** is a safe place for people to see wild animals and learn more about them.